Grammar for Literacy

Year 6

David Orme

Introduction

The photocopiable pages in this book, and the accompanying teachers' notes, provide support and source material for the DfEE document *Grammar for Writing*. They can also be used independently as a complete course in the essentials of grammar in the context of writing for years 3 to 6.

Principles

Traditionally, grammar has been taught through exercises, usually single sentences illustrating the particular grammatical point. Teachers have found that teaching grammar in this way, without a meaningful context, is unlikely to be as successful as teaching grammar within the context of the children's own reading and writing. However, that approach too has its own problems – waiting for a grammatical point to arise from work in progress makes any systematic teaching of the subject difficult.

This series attempts to provide the context for looking at grammar by providing a lively selection of short but complete texts – fiction, non-fiction and poetry – which have been specially written to illustrate the key points. The notes provide suggestions for teaching strategies, and a range of writing tasks to reinforce children's understanding. The focus of the activities is entirely on writing; other reinforcement activities, and background for teachers on the grammatical issues, are covered very thoroughly in the *Grammar for Writing* document.

Using the materials

The materials are designed both for whole-class presentation and for group and individual work. The writing activities can be used flexibly – the guided writing should involve a teacher or other adult, and can be done with the whole class or in a group. The independent writing activities are suitable for small groups, children working in pairs, or individuals.

In some cases additional texts are provided in the teachers' notes, and preparation may be needed before the session starts.

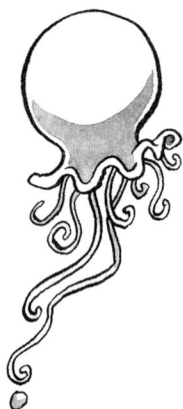

Contents

Topic

1 Revision of Word Classes

GfW unit covered: 44
Objective: S1 (Term 1)
Grammar or language topics covered:

- Word classes and their functions
- Word choice
- Use of similes
- Word choice in different types of text.

● ●

Session 1

This session should cover verbs and verb modifiers, including:

★ use of interesting verbs;

★ avoidance of auxiliary verbs (verb chains);

★ function of adverbs;

★ adverbial phrases.

Whole class
Read passage 1 *Alien Arrival* with the class, pointing out adverbs and adverbial phrases, e.g. gradually, about, at last, out, very, silently, when the main force arrived.

List adverbs under their functions, e.g. how (gradually, silently), when (at last, already, when the main force arrived), where (out), intensity (very, quite).

Discuss how a group of words can perform the function of an adverb.

Reinforce the idea that adverbs change or describe verbs; additionally, show how they can change or describe adjectives or other adverbs, e.g. very tall, quite easily.

Point out verb chains, e.g. 'were glowing', 'was gradually opening'. Discuss the differences between 'were glowing' and 'glowed', 'was opening' and 'opened' – auxiliary verbs can make the writing less powerful.

Shared writing
Look at the verb choices that refer to the aliens - moving, looking, stepped, and so on. Work together to find more interesting substitutes.

Independent writing
Ask children to continue the extract, describing the actions of the aliens upon reaching the town. Explain that they will score a point for every interesting verb and for every adverb or adverbial phrase used.

Session 2

This session should cover nouns and noun modifiers, including:

★ noun phrases;

★ adjectives and adjectival phrases;

★ prepositional phrases;

★ similes.

Whole class

Look at passage 1 again, this time pointing out a selection of noun phrases (e.g. 'quiet valley outside town', 'glow in the sky'), adjectives (e.g. strange, mysterious), prepositions and the nouns they qualify (e.g. *outside* town, *on* very long necks, *to* each other) and the simile 'like the whispering of a breeze through the branches of a tree'.

• Identify nouns and noun phrases that are the subject of a sentence.
• Discuss the choice of adjectives and possible substitutes.
• Show how prepositions always come before the noun they modify, e.g. into the sky.
• Identify and discuss the simile, reminding children that similes are comparisons beginning with 'like' or 'as', and can be used as an alternative to or can extend an adverb or an adjective.

Shared writing

Look at one or two of the pieces of work produced as individual writing in session 1. Discuss how interesting similes could be used to make the descriptions more vivid.

Independent writing

Ask children to redraft their individual pieces of writing, scoring points for replacing prosaic adjectives with more interesting ones, and using similes instead of adjectives or adverbs. Stress that it is important not to overuse similes.

Session 3

This session should cover:

★ adapting texts for particular purposes;

★ use of imperative verbs;

★ use of the present tense;

★ use of 'official' language.

Whole class

Read passage 2 *A Warning to Householders* to the class, discussing the key differences between this and passage 1, i.e. although it is clearly fiction it is written in the style of a non-fiction, instructional text, and therefore uses the present tense and the imperative mood. The style is 'mock official'. The humour comes from the contrast between the gravity of the style and the absurdity of the content. The sentences are shorter, to give extra clarity. Numbers are used to show a sequenced activity.

Discuss how this information would be presented, e.g. a notice in a newspaper, a poster, (perhaps stuck on lampposts!) or a leaflet pushed through a door.

Shared writing

Discuss another crisis situation that would require a similar emergency notice. Model a poster or leaflet that might be sent out by the authorities.

Independent writing

Either ask children to create their posters based on the writing model worked on in the shared writing activity, or devise their own scenario requiring a warning poster.

Topic

2 Active and Passive

GfW unit covered: 45
Objectives: S2 and S3 (Term 1)
Grammar or language topics covered:

• Active and passive verbs
(Note: some of the writing produced in this topic can be used for Topic 6 so should be retained.)

• •

Session 1

This session should cover:
★ revision of subject and object.

Whole class
Read passage 1 *A Tense Task* (1) to the class, pointing out every occurrence of the word 'by'.

Remind children of the typical sentence structure, i.e. subject (who or what did it), verb (what was done), object (who or what had it done to them). This is called the active voice – it describes an action, e.g. 'Mrs Smith glared angrily at the class'.

Recap with the children that, while all sentences have a subject and verb, not all will have an object, e.g. 'Mrs Smith glared angrily'.

Explain that the sentence can be changed so that the person or thing that has something done to them – e.g. the class, can become the subject of the sentence – 'the class was glared at by an angry Mrs Smith'. This structure is called the passive voice, and a clue that it is being used is the word 'by'.

Like the active voice, a sentence in the passive voice does not need an object – 'the class was glared at' – but here the word 'by' is omitted.

Shared writing
Select three examples of passive sentences from the passage. Write them out using different colours for the object, verb, subject, and a further colour for the word 'by'.

Work on three new, linked sentences using the passive voice. Keep them as simple as possible, e.g. 'The letters were being delivered by the postman', 'The postman was bitten by the dog', 'The dog was reported to the police'. (Note that the last sentence does not have an object.)

Independent writing
Ask children to write their own linked passive sentences, using the model from the shared writing.

This session should cover:

★ changing active to passive.

Whole class

Read passage 2 *A Tense Task (2)* to the class, then reread passage 1. The children will notice that many of the sentences in passage 2 have been switched round, i.e. are using the active voice.

Discuss the effect of using the active and passive. Why is the first sentence active in both passages? Try and make a passive version, i.e. 'the window was looked through by Abdel'. Why didn't the author use this?

Find other active sentences from passage 1, e.g. 'Abdel strolled into the shop . . .'. Why wouldn't this work in the passive?

Discuss which parts of which text sound the most 'natural'.

Shared writing

Write up some of the sentences created in the session 1 shared and independent writing activities. Work with the class to turn them into active sentences.

Independent writing

Ask children to work on reworking passage 1 into the active voice, using passage 2 and the work done in the shared writing activity as a model.

Session 3

This session should cover:

★ using both active and passive within a text.

Whole class

In teaching the use of the passive voice, it is important to stress:
• The active voice is more commonly used.
• The passive voice is useful to give variety to writing, or when the writer wishes to emphasise that somebody or something had something done to them, e.g. 'Mum was frightened by a spider'.

Read passage 3 *One Thing After Another* to the class. This is mainly written in the passive voice. Some sentences work best in the passive, by creating suspense, but others sound awkward, e.g. 'Once the office had been reached by Vicki . . .'.

Shared writing

Work with the class to rewrite the passage, using a mixture of the active and the passive voice, deciding in each case which would be the most suitable. (Note: if possible, this work should be retained for use in Topic 6.)

Independent writing

Ask children to use passage 3 as a model for writing about 'a bad day' in the first person, e.g. a difficult breakfast, trouble getting to school, problems at school. Explain that they should attempt to use a mixture of active and passive sentences.

Topic 3 Connectives in Different Text Types

GfW unit covered: 46
Objective: S4 (Term 1)
Grammar or language topics covered:

• Different functions of connectives

(Note: some of the writing produced in this topic can be used for Topic 4 so should be retained.)

●●●

Session 1

This session should cover:
★ revision of connectives.

Whole class
Copy out the following pairs of sentences:

The rain stopped. She took off her coat.
The cat was old and slow. It caught a mouse.
The bus broke down. Charles was late for school.

Explain that the class is going to work together to join the sentences using connectives. Some sentences may sound more sensible than others, e.g. 'Although the rain stopped, she took off her coat' is not as sensible as 'Once the rain stopped, she took off her coat'.

Look for connectives that give different meanings, e.g. 'Before the rain stopped, she took off her coat', 'Because the rain stopped she took off her coat'.

Include conjunctions that come between the sentences, e.g. so, and, but, then, until. Try each one in turn. List the connectives tried. Use the DfEE's *Grammar for Writing* (*GfW*) document (Page 130) for further suggestions.

Discuss the function of the various connectives, e.g. to show time (before, first, once, next, etc), reason or consequence (because, so, therefore, etc), linking opposite or conflicting ideas (although, however, etc) or adding another idea (and, also).

Shared writing
Choose the 'best version' of one of the linked sentences to start a short piece of writing using a range of connectives, e.g. 'Although the cat was old and slow, it caught a mouse. Once it had killed it with a blow from its paw, it hid it in a corner of the living room. A week later . . .'.

Independent writing
Ask children either to continue with the writing started in the shared writing session, or to begin a new piece based on one of the other sentences. Explain that they will score one point for each connective used, two points if it starts the sentence.

This session should cover:

★ connectives showing a range of functions.

Whole class

Read passage 1 *Mrs Turner's Plan*. Discuss the humour of the passage before starting on the work on its grammar.

Point out the connectives before, so, although, and, once, next, as soon as, after this, finally, and discuss the function of the various connectives, e.g. time (once), consequence (so), linking conflicting ideas (although) and adding a further idea (and).

Point out that a semi-colon has been used to replace a connective at one point: '. . . the right quantity into it; sieving made her cakes lighter'. What connective could be used instead?

Discuss how connectives could be used to link any two of the first three sentences.

Shared writing

Create a writing frame showing a time sequence, listing connectives which could be used to link prior, concurrent and subsequent actions, e.g. before, first, next, at the same time, then, finally, afterwards.

Discuss various scenarios for writing using this frame, e.g. planning and carrying out a surprise birthday party, or even a bank robbery!

Independent writing

Ask children to use the writing frame and one of the scenarios discussed (or one of their own devising) to produce a piece of writing.

Session 3

This session should cover:

★ connectives in non-fiction text.

Whole class

Read passage 2 *How to Build a Website*, asking children to identify connectives.

Discuss the main difference between passages 1 and 2, i.e. both describe a process but one is descriptive, the other instructional. Remind children of the function of the imperative, e.g. 'create a home page'.

Discuss the function of the connectives despite, however, because, when.

Discuss the various purposes of passage 2, i.e. to persuade the reader that a website is important, to convince them that what they thought would be difficult is really quite easy, and to provide a simple outline of how to go about creating a website.

Shared writing.

Use this model to plan a further piece of writing, e.g. to persuade someone that keeping crocodiles is a good idea and easy to achieve, giving an instructional overview. This may or may not involve a time sequence.

Independent writing

Ask children to fill out the model worked on in the shared writing activity. More confident children could create their own scenario.

Topic 4 More Punctuation

GfW unit covered: 47

Objectives: S5 and S6 (Term 1), S3 (Term 2), S4 Term 3)

Grammar or language topics covered:

• Colons
• Semi-colons
• Commas
• Dashes
• Brackets

• •

Session 1

This session should cover:

★ semi-colons;

★ colons.

Whole class

Read passage 1 *An Obituary* and discuss the function of an obituary.

Point out colons and semi-colons, discussing their function, i.e. colons introduce lists and quotations; semi-colons take the place of connectives.

For each semi-colon, discuss possible connectives, e.g. 'because he was always looking…', '…and we shall all miss him'.

Explain that using a semi-colon instead of a connective adds variety to writing; it can mean that 'and' is used less. It also helps the reader by inserting a longer pause at important moments.

Shared writing

Return to the paired sentences looked at in Topic 3 (see page 6). Discuss which of these could be joined with a semi-colon. ('The cat was old and slow; it caught a mouse' does not work because one sentence is not a consequence of the other - a word such as 'although' is needed to make a logical connection.)

Independent writing

Ask children to revise one of their pieces of independent writing from Topic 3, looking to see which conjunctions could sensibly be replaced by a semi-colon. Alternatively, they could rework passage 1 or 2 from Topic 3.

This session should cover:

★ dashes;

★ brackets;

★ commas used to cut off part of a sentence.

Whole class

Reread passage 1, highlighting statements enclosed in commas (e.g. in the first sentence), in dashes and in brackets.

Read the sentences aloud, with and without the parenthetical (separated) sections, showing that they are not necessary for the sense of the sentence – the effect is of temporarily leaving the sentence, then coming back to it. The three ways shown in the passage differ by degree, with commas being the weakest, brackets the strongest. Dashes are often considered rather informal and would not be considered appropriate for an obituary, though they are increasingly used in formal writing.

Shared writing

Model sentences using commas, dashes and brackets. They can be used to provide further information about a subject, e.g. 'Mr Jones, the headmaster of the school, . . .', 'Tom, a black and white cat, was sleeping. . .', 'John – one of the real nuisances in the class – laughed loudly'. Brackets are often used to explain the meaning of a word, or a difficult idea, e.g. 'Rubella (German measles) is currently rife . . .' as well as separating a whole sentence from the rest of a passage. Discuss how the dashes and brackets add extra emphasis. Deciding between three options is a matter of emphasis, style and ensuring variety in writing.

Independent writing

Ask children to use one of the sentences produced in shared writing activity in a short piece of writing, including at least one further example of commas used to separate out a section of a sentence. Work on commas is the most useful; more able children could include dashes and brackets.

Session 3

This session should cover:

★ revision of punctuation.

Whole class

Read passage 2 *Mad About Manchester*, which is poorly punctuated. Discuss any possible uses for question or exclamation marks, decide where speech marks should be used and discuss where a full stop could be used instead of a comma. Identify a list that should be introduced with a colon and highlight any parenthetical phrases.

Shared writing

Work with the class on a redraft of the first two sentences, reworking the punctuation and deciding whether parenthetical commas should be replaced by dashes or brackets.

Independent writing

Now ask children to complete the redrafting task, bearing in mind the discussion in the whole-class session.

Topic 5 Complex Sentences

GfW unit covered: 47
Objectives: S5 and S6 (Term 1), S3 (Term 2), S4 Term 3)
Grammar or language topics covered:

• Forming complex sentences using a range of connective devices
• Checking clarity in complex sentences
• Exploring meaning through position of clauses

(Note: some of the writing produced in this topic can be used for Topic 9 so should be retained.)

● ●

Session 1

This session should cover:

★ means of connecting sentences – participles, phrases.

Whole class
Passage 1 *Ready, Steady, GO!* contains a wide range of connective devices, i.e.
• using an '-ing' word (participle), e.g. 'wiping the sweat . . .';
• using an adverb, e.g. tensely;
• using a range of conjunctions, some showing time sequences;
• using a connective to create a compound sentence;
• using a semi-colon instead of a connective
and, (an important option):
• keeping the sentence short and simple!

Discuss some or all of these choices, illustrating them with examples from the text.

Shared writing
Work with the class to change the sentences in the passage using different devices, e.g.
'Straining and sweating, the two teams . . .'
'Shamefacedly, Great Puddington . . .'
'Great Puddington dug their heels in desperately, but nearer and nearer . . .'
'. . . had moved into the village; hopes were high . . .'

Independent writing
Ask children to create their own sentences, using as many connecting devices as possible. (These will be used for the work in session 2.)

This session should cover:

★ clause order.

Whole class

This session focuses on the order of the clauses within the sentences in passage 1. Work through the text, changing the order of clauses and discussing the difference this makes. 'The two teams in the final stared at each other, wiping sweat off their faces' is obviously confusing, 'Great Puddington were determined to make it four in a row and had won for the last three years' is obviously unsatisfactory. In most other cases, it will be a matter of style and emphasis, e.g. which is better: 'Great Puddington slunk away, ashamed and humiliated', or 'Ashamed and humiliated, Great Puddington slunk away', or do they have exactly the same force?

Shared writing

Pick two sentences – 'Nearer and nearer to the all-important line moved the ribbon' would be a good choice for one – and work on all possibilities for arrangement.

Independent writing

Ask children to work on rearranging the sentences they wrote for the independent writing activity in session 1, seeing which rearrangements work and which do not.

Session 3

This session should cover:

★ revision of complex sentences.

Whole class

Look at passage 2 *A Crisis at the Zoo* with the class. Explain that the session's task is to rewrite this text to make an interesting and varied piece of writing.

Write up a list of options, such as:
• simple sentences;
• complex sentences joined with a connective at the beginning;
• complex sentences linked by a connective between them;
• joining clauses with an 'ing' word (participle);
• rearranging the sentences in a more interesting order;
• putting ideas in the middle of a sentence, using commas or dashes.

Shared writing

Begin to work through the passage with the class. Stress that short sentences are not bad sentences – they can be very effective, especially when the story gets exciting! Stress also that the words and order of the text can been changed as much as the children wish, as long as it makes sense, e.g. they could try starting with 'The keepers stared in horror. With one bound, the lion had escaped from the truck bringing it to the zoo'. Discuss whether speech marks would make the passage more interesting, e.g. "We need people with dart guns – now!"

Independent writing

Ask the children to complete, and possibly extend, the rewriting of passage 2. This writing will be used again in Topic 9.

Topic 6 · Further Work on Active and Passive

GfW unit covered: 48
Objectives: S1 (Term 2) and S3 (Term 3)
Grammar or language topics covered:

- Revision of the passive voice
- Use of the concealed passive

• •

Session 1

This session should cover:

★ revision of active and passive.

Whole class
Return to passages 1 and 2 of Topic 2. Remind children of the key differences between active and passive outlined there, if possible by looking again additionally at the writing produced in session 3 of Topic 2.

Shared writing
Work together on the short sentences in passage 2 of Topic 5. Look at the first four sentences, deciding which could be rewritten in the passive voice, e.g. 'It was being brought the zoo by the truck', 'It was stared at by the zoo keepers', 'A mobile phone was snatched up by . . .'

Independent writing
Ask children, perhaps working in groups, to select further sentences from the escaped lion text, and rewrite them in the passive voice.

Session 2

This session should cover:

★ use of the disguised passive.

Whole class
The children will be familiar with the structure of a simple passive sentence, e.g. 'the man was hit by a brick'. Before reading passage 1 *Susan's Good Idea,* introduce the idea of the passive sentence in which we do not know who or what did the deed, e.g. 'the man was hit on the head' and the passive sentence that has no object, e.g. 'the journey was finished'.

Work through passage 1. Discuss sentences where the object or agent is clear, e.g. 'the problem had been caused by a derailment' and those using the concealed passive, discussing who did it, e.g. Who told the passengers? - the guard on the train. What made the passengers furious? - the delay. Who hired the bus? - the rail company.

Look also for sentences with no 'agent', e.g. 'the interview was timed for 2.30'.

Shared writing

Begin work on a short diary or journal extract in which the diary writer, e.g. an explorer, describes what has happened to him/her on the previous day, e.g. "I was knocked down, then tied up with a strong rope. I was hauled along a jungle track by the monsters, and…".

Independent writing

Ask children to continue the journal entry, scoring points for interesting and effective use of the passive voice.

Session 3

This session should cover:

★ using the passive voice in poetry.

Whole class

Share the poem *Old House in the Hills* with the class, initially discussing its content and use of imagery and language. Ensure children understand any difficult words or ideas.

Identify the use of the passive voice, and discuss why this is particularly effective in a description of something like an old house, battered by the elements.

Shared writing

Discuss other scenarios where the subject of the poem is a victim of passing time, e.g. an old person, a closed factory, a steam engine or car in a scrap yard, a fallen tree.

Work together to build a framework for the poem, with words, ideas and images. (Using the same alliterative opening is a possibility.)

Independent writing

Now ask children to use the material from the shared writing activity to produce a first draft of their poem. Remind them that the poem should be written mainly in the passive voice.

Topic

7 Official Language

GfW unit covered: 49
Objectives: S2 (Term 2) and S3 (Term 3)
Grammar or language topics covered:

• Formal and informal writing

● ●

Session 1

This session should cover:

★ elements of a formal letter.

Whole class

Read text 1 *A Reminder (1)*. First, point out the formatting points on an official letter, e.g. the positioning of the addresses, the style of address and the 'Yours sincerely' closure. ('Yours faithfully' as an ending is in decline, although it is still used for Dear Sir/Madam openings.)

Discuss why a reference number is often used in an official letter.

Discuss the tone of the letter, highlighting words and phrases that seem particularly formal or over formal, e.g. 'communication' rather than 'letter', 'sufficient funds' rather than 'enough money', 'respectfully advise' (how respectful is the letter?).

Compare this letter with text 2 *A Reminder (2)*. Why would this letter be inappropriate?

Shared writing

Explain that the object of the independent writing activity is to rewrite the letter from Wessex Power in a clearer and less formal manner which is still polite to the person receiving it. Pompous phrases should be rewritten, e.g. 'If sufficient funds are not forthcoming. . . .' could read 'if the bill is not paid in seven days'. Provide a template and key words for this letter.

Independent writing

Ask children to produce a correctly set out version of the letter planned in the shared writing activity.

Session 2

This session should cover:

★ writing a semi-formal letter.

Whole class

Read through the independent writing produced in session 1. Discuss how successful the children were at reducing the formality of text 1.

Now explain to the class that they are going to work on a semi-formal letter to a teacher in their next school. This might be their prospective form tutor or year head. Discuss how formal such a letter should be, e.g. how it should be opened and closed.

Shared writing

Discuss the content of such a letter, e.g. introducing the writer, saying how much they are looking forward to coming to the school, and asking any questions about the new school.

Draft an outline of the letter with the class.

Independent writing

Ask children to produce the letter planned in the shared writing activity.

Session 3

This session should cover:

★ informal writing.

Whole class

Read the following letter with the children and compare the format and tone with passage 1 and the writing produced in session 2. Pick out words and phrases that show informality, e.g. the informal opening and close, and the use of slang.

15 Bank Street
Bournemouth
Tues.

Dear Mike,

     Just a quick note to remind you of the thirty quid you still owe me. Remember? I lent you some dosh last month when you were a bit skint, so you could get those CDs you were after. It's time you coughed up, mate! I wouldn't ask but I'm a bit short myself this month – the holiday cost more than I thought, then I needed a new tyre on the motor – you know how it is. A cheque would be OK, but if you could let me have cash that would be brilliant. £30.64 was the exact amount, but I'm not bothered about the 64p.

     Hope everything's OK with you, old friend. Last time I drove past your place everything was dark, but I thought I saw a candle flickering inside. Perhaps you were having a power cut.

     Anyway, hurry along with the readies, mate, and I'll see you around.
Cheers

Tony

List slang words and expressions, putting the 'correct' version next to them. Would slang be appropriate in the letter to a new teacher? Why not?

Shared writing

Ask children to imagine that Mike borrowed the money not from his friend Tony but from an elderly (but friendly) aunt who now needs her money back. Plan out the letter that she might write.

Independent writing
Ask children to write the aunt's letter.

Topic 8 Contracting Sentences, Note Making

GfW unit covered: 50
Objective: S4 (Term 2)
Grammar or language topics covered:

- Note making from chronological and non-chronological texts
- Using timelines

● ●

Session 1

This session should cover:

★ note making from a chronological text.

(Note: if possible, allow a few days to elapse between note making and reworking a text.)

Whole class

Discuss with the class the reasons why note making is an important skill, i.e. it is useful to be able to extract information quickly from a book or other resource, pick out the key points from a talk or provide someone with information in a quick, easy-to-read form. The technique is to keep the sense using as few words as possible.

Read but do not show passage 2 from Topic 3, *How to Build a Website*. Explain that, in the shared writing activity, the class will be working together to list the main points on website building in order – they must listen carefully! Now read the text a second time.

Shared writing

Explain that the class is only going to note down the things someone needs to do to build a website – the opening paragraph can therefore be ignored. The notes should end up something like this:

1. Use a web-designing programme to make a home page.
2. Create more pages.
3. Link them to your home page.
4. Find a host for your website
5. Upload your pages using an FTP program.

Independent writing

Ask children (perhaps working in pairs) to use numbered notes to give instructions for a journey. This could be an imaginative piece of writing, e.g. how get through the haunted wood alive, how to locate a pirate's treasure. Alternatively, ask them to write notes on a current piece of work in history, geography, or another subject. The notes must be as brief as possible.

Session 2

This session should cover:

★ timelines.

Whole class

Read passage 1 *The History of the Parachute* with the class, highlighting the dates. Then look at text 2 *Parachute Timeline*. Discuss why a timeline is a good format for making notes from passage 1.

Discuss anything that has been missed out from the timeline, e.g. the information in the first paragraph. Why couldn't this be included?

Discuss the use of abbreviations in note making to save time and space.

Shared writing

Look again at text 2 from Topic 2, *One Thing After Another*. With the class rewrite this as a timeline, putting in hours and minutes instead of years, e.g. '7.28 Broke plate. 7.30 Got told off by Mum'.

Independent writing

Ask children to use the timeline formula to write an account of a day, using as much imagination as possible! (Note: these accounts could be expanded into a recounted text in an extended writing session.)

Session 3

This session should cover:

★ non-chronological note making.

Whole class

Explain to the class that the object of this session is to produce notes from texts that are not chronological, i.e. the order in which the information is given is not so important. As in the shared writing activity for session 2, key headings will be used instead.

Shared writing

Read text 1 again. Discuss an alternative strategy for writing notes about the parachute – the use of headings. Identify key headings for notes, e.g. experiments with parachutes, parachute design, parachutes in war time, parachutes today. Make notes under these headings. Compare the two approaches, headings and timelines. Which is better?

Independent writing

Ask the class to reread passage 1 from Topic 4 – the obituary. Explain that they have to write an entry for Sir James Carstairs in a dictionary of biography. They will need to include an introductory sentence, headings, then the information in note form. The entry should be as short as possible. If there is time, discuss possible headings, e.g. exploring achievements, character, later achievements and honours.

Topic 9 Summary

GfW units covered: 50
Objective: S4 (Term 2)
Grammar or language topics covered:

• Summarising fiction, real events, longer texts

● ●

Session 1

This session should cover:

★ summarising fiction.

Whole class
Read passage 1 *At the End of the Day (1)*, then passage 2. Explain that passage 2 is a summary of passage 1, i.e. it gives the important points only, but in complete sentences.

Discuss the uses of summary, e.g. in newspaper accounts and encyclopaedia entries. Explain that the most important task is deciding what to leave in and what to leave out. Discuss how well passage 2 has achieved this. Has anything important been left out?

Shared writing
Revisit the independent writing done in session 3 of Topic 5, selecting one piece of text from those written by the children. Alternatively use passage 2 from Topic 5. Work through the text together, picking out key points, e.g. 'A lion escaped from a truck on the way to the zoo. The head keeper rang to ask for people with dart guns. They were busy...'

Independent writing
Either ask children to complete the task started in the shared writing session, or to summarise a new text such as Topic 5 passage 1, or Topic 6 passage 1.

Session 2

This session should cover:

★ summarising a real event.

Whole class
Discuss a real event that the class has been involved in recently. This could be something quite simple, such as a morning assembly, a sports event, or even the previous day's lessons! Make a list of the key things that happened as part of that event.

Shared writing
Begin work on writing a newspaper account. Start by deciding on a suitable headline, e.g. 'A hard-working day for class 6' and a sub-headline, 'Good progress made, claims teacher'. Devise a summarising first sentence, e.g. 'Class 6 of Lakeside school were put through their paces in numeracy, literacy and science yesterday'.

Independent writing

Ask the class to complete the summary, including only key information.

This session should cover:

★ summarising a longer text.

Whole class

Children find the task of summarising a novel, film or TV programme difficult, as they tend to become bogged down in unnecessary detail. This is often because they fail to note down key points and organise their thoughts in advance.

Work together on as short a version as possible of a text the children are familiar with, e.g. 'Harry Potter discovered he was a wizard. He went to a school for wizards called Hogwarts. Harry's greatest enemy was an evil wizard called Voldemort, who had killed Harry's parents. Harry fought and defeated Voldemort.'

Shared writing

Work together on a summary of a different medium such as a film, e.g. 'A scientist found a way to recreate dinosaurs. He built a zoo on an island . . .'.

Independent writing

Ask children to produce brief summaries of their own, perhaps covering a range of media.

Topic 10 Conditionals

GfW unit covered: 51
Objective: S5 (Term 2)
Grammar or language topics covered:

• Use of the conditional

Session 1

This session should cover:

★ introduction to conditionals.

Whole class

Start by writing the first parts of some conditional sentences on the board, e.g.
If you leave the window open at night . . .
Unless it stops raining very soon . . .
I would accept what you say if . . .
Ask for a range of endings for the sentences.

Explain that these are conditional sentences, based on the structure 'if this . . . then that'.
Conditional sentences use conjunctions such as 'if', 'as long as' and 'unless'.

Read through passage 1 *How to Look After Your Qrrp*, and identify conditional structures. Note that
the first sentence of paragraph 3 is not conditional; how could it be made into a conditional sentence?
(One possibility is 'If your pet is furry, it will need grooming, but Qrrps . . .'.)

Shared writing

Use the model of passage 1 to begin a similar piece on a more conventional pet, or on choosing the
best pet. Create a range of conditional sentences, e.g. 'Don't choose a dog unless you are prepared
to take it for a walk every day', 'A budgie will be happy as long as it has plenty of food and water.'

Independent writing

Ask children to use the sentences created in the shared writing session, and further sentences of
their own, to write a complete text.

This session should cover:

★ putting forward an argument – if . . . then.

Whole class
Explain to the class that conditional sentences are often used to put forward a point of view, e.g. 'Unless we stop polluting the world, the human race has no future', 'If we didn't have to go to school, life would be much more fun', 'As long as we go on coming to school by car, the traffic congestion will not improve.'

Ask the class to invent a conditional sentence putting forward a point of view. They do not necessarily have to agree with the statements they make, and they can be as absurd as they wish, e.g. 'If everyone painted their faces green, they could hide from the teachers in the long grass.'

Shared writing
Plan a piece of writing putting forward a point of view, perhaps extending one of the ideas from the whole-class session. Work on a least three conditional sentences, using different conjunctions.

Independent writing
Ask children to use the conditional sentences, and others of their own, to complete the work started in the shared writing activity.

Session 3

This session should cover:

★ conditional poems.

Whole class
Read the poem *A Sulky Girl Wishes She Was the Sun*. Discuss the ways in which the sun can appear to behave like a sulky person. How would the poem change if the title was 'A cheerful girl wishes she was the sun'? Discuss this alternative version.

Discuss the form of the poem. Each stanza is just one complex sentence, each containing two conditional ideas.

Discuss other ideas for using this poetry pattern, e.g. If I were the rain/wind/night/sea/prime minister; If I were a volcano/aeroplane/teacher.

Shared writing
Select one of the ideas from the whole-class session and work on a class poem using the structure.

Independent writing
Ask children to use the structure for a conditional poem of their own.

Topic
11 Paragraph Structures

GfW unit covered: 52
Objective: T2 (Term 2)
Grammar or language topics covered:

- Structuring individual paragraphs in fiction and non-fiction

● ●

Session 1

This session should cover:

★ introduction to using paragraphs in fiction.

Whole class

Read passage 1 *Worried Sick*, looking closely at the paragraph sequence. Construct a table giving details of the paragraphs, e.g. (1) what was happening at home; (2) the feelings of Tara's parents; (3) Tara struggling to get home; (4) the situation later at home. Discuss the reasons for changing to a new paragraph, e.g. a change of time, place or subject, and the beginning of direct speech.

Identify paragraph openers that explain the new time, setting, or subject, e.g. 'meanwhile', 'back at home'.

Shared writing

Discuss the possible content of a new first paragraph, ending with 'Dad paced up and down the room. Why couldn't children do what they were told?' What could be the setting and subject matter? What would be a good opening sentence?

Independent writing

Divide the children into two groups. Ask one group to write the opening paragraph, based on the planning in the shared writing session. Ask the other group to complete the final paragraph, e.g. describing what happened after Tara's parents heard a noise outside the door.

Session 2

This session should cover:

★ writing summaries of paragraphs;

★ planning a paragraph sequence;

★ writing paragraphs.

Whole class

Read through selected versions of the completed story about Tara. Evaluate the various versions produced, and select a final version.

Shared writing

Write a summary (see Topic 9) of one of the paragraphs, e.g. 'Tara was walking home. She had missed the bus and her phone had a flat battery. She was worried about what her parents would do when she got home.'

Work with the children on a five-paragraph narrative sequence; alternatively, use the following:
1. Tara (or a different character) has been saving for something she specially wanted. Her parents have given her money to make up the amount.
2. She sets off on the bus, feeling really excited.
3. When she gets to the shops, she discovers she has lost her purse! How can she tell her parents that the money is lost?
4. Her parents receive a phone call from the bus company – the purse, with address and phone number, has been handed in!
5. She starts the long walk home – Dad, driving the car, meets her on the way with the good news.

Independent writing

Ask children to write up one of the paragraphs in full. The finished paragraphs can be combined to make various versions of the same story.

Session 3

This session should cover:

★ paragraphs in non-fiction.

Whole class

Read paragraphs 1 and 2 of passage 2 *Late Night Bus Services*. Discuss the differences between passages 1 and 2. Although passage 2 could appear in a story as fiction it is written in the style of information writing, with paragraph headings instead of paragraph openers. Discuss what openers could be used instead, e.g. 'Punctuality is very poor'.

Discuss paragraph 3, which has not been completed and is in note form.

Shared writing

Work together to expand paragraph 3 to match the other paragraphs.

Discuss a 'rounding off' paragraph in which the writer might state an overall opinion of the bus services, demand a reply, and perhaps threaten to take his or her complaints further – or even take some sort of direct action.

Independent writing

Ask children to write the final paragraph, based on the work done in the shared writing activity.

Topic

12 Recounted Text

GfW units covered: 53

Objective: S1 (Term 3)

Grammar or language topics covered:

- Recount through journal writing
- Recount in non-fiction writing

● ●

Session 1

This session should cover:

★ using recount in the form of a journal.

Whole class

Read passage 1 *Judy's Journal* with the class. This is an example of fiction using forms of non-fiction, in this case, a journal.

Discuss the differences between a diary and a journal, i.e. although the words can be used interchangeably (q.v. Samuel Pepys' diary) in modern usage a diary is a book in which you can list future events, and make brief notes about what has happened. A journal is a more likely to be written in continuous prose.

If possible, share extracts from historical diaries/journals, e.g. Pepys' diary, Daniel Defoe's *Journal of the Plague Year* (which is partly fictional).

Discuss why journals will always be written in the first person. What are the differences between a journal and an autobiography?

Shared writing

Discuss what might happen next in passage 1, and plan out further paragraphs.

Independent writing

Ask children to work up the plans from the shared writing session into completed paragraphs.

Session 2

This session should cover:

★ non-fiction recount.

(Note: prepare in advance key facts about an explorer such as Neil Armstrong or Captain Cook.)

Whole class

Read passage 2 *The Story of Christopher Columbus*. Discuss the similarities and differences between this and passage 1, i.e. passage 2 describes chronological events in the past tense, but is written in the third person, with no direct speech.

Shared writing

Introduce and list your key facts about another explorer. Explain that the children are going to work up these facts into a piece of recounted writing.

Discuss what facts will feature in each paragraph, and how the text will be introduced and concluded.

Independent writing

Ask children to work on their recount text about the explorer.

Session 3

This session should cover:

★ changing a third-person recount into the form of a journal.

Whole class

Return to passage 2. Ask the children to imagine that Christopher Columbus's long lost journal has just been discovered. How would it be written? What worries would Columbus be having? How would he write about them in his journal? How would he feel when land was finally sighted?

Shared writing

Work together to write the entries for October 11th and 12th, 1492.

Independent writing

Ask children now to rework their 'explorer' texts from session 2, turning them into journals.

Topic 13 Features of Instructional Texts

GfW unit covered: 53
Objective: S1 (Term 3)
Grammar or language topics covered:

- Instructional texts showing a time sequence
- Non-chronological instructions

- -

Session 1

This session should cover:

★ chronological instructional texts.

Whole class
Read through passage 1 *How to Use an Internet Search Engine*. Identify the opening paragraph outlining the information in the whole text.

Discuss why the author chose to use numbers rather than bullet points.

Identify words showing a time sequence, e.g. now, once you have. Discuss whether using the word 'first' would be useful for the second paragraph, or whether the numbering makes this unnecessary.

Identify examples of the use of the imperative.

Discuss why the text is written in short sentences, many of them simple sentences.

Shared writing
Plan out a further piece of 'how to' chronological writing, based on a familiar task, e.g. how to make a telephone call from a phone box, or how to send a text message using a mobile phone.

Independent writing
Ask children to write their instructional text, based on the work in the shared writing session. More confident children could write instructional texts from scratch.

Session 2

This session should cover:

★ non-chronological instructions.

Whole class
Read passage 2 *How to Attract Wild Birds to Your Garden*, discussing the key differences between it and passage 1, i.e. it is not set out in numbered paragraphs and the sentences are longer.

Discuss whether the instructions are chronological. Does it matter in which order the instructions are carried out, or do they all need to happen together? Would missing out one instruction, e.g. providing water, mean that no birds would come at all? What would be the effect of missing out instruction 2 in passage 1?

Shared writing

Discuss how passage 2 could be written to look more like passage 1, summarising and using bullet points and shorter sentences, e.g. 'Make sure birds have supply of water to drink'.

Independent writing

Ask children to rework passage 2 using bullet points, as planned during the shared writing session.

Session 3

This session should cover:

★ structuring instructional writing by order of importance.

Whole class

Look again at passage 2. Note use of time sequence words, e.g. first, next. Do these activities (discouraging cats, providing cover) need to be done in this order, or do the words indicate something else, i.e. relative importance – discouraging cats being the most important, providing cover the next most important? Why might discouraging cats be the most important instruction?

Discuss other possible non-chronological instructions, e.g. how to tidy a bedroom. Are there any elements that would need to be done chronologically, e.g. tidying the floor before using a vacuum clear? What might be the most important things to remember?

Shared writing

Work on a series of instructions for using a swimming pool, ranging from important safety considerations (e.g. do not use the pool unless there is qualified adult supervision) to less important ones (e.g. leave the changing room tidy).

Independent writing

Ask children to produce a notice for a swimming pool, using the instructions discussed in the shared writing activity. Explain that the instructions should be logical (i.e. all instructions to do with the changing room should be put together) but the most important instructions (safety) should come first. Use bullet points. Are there any other ways that the most important instructions could be highlighted?

Topic

14 Persuasive and Discursive Texts

GfW unit covered: 53
Objective: S1 (Term 3)
Grammar or language topics covered:

• Writing discursive texts, setting out both sides of an argument
• Writing texts putting forward a point of view
(Note: work done on conditionals (Topic 10) would be useful revision before tackling this topic.)

• •

Session 1

This session should cover:

★ introducing a simple model for discursive writing.

Whole class
Introduce the idea of a simple 'for and against' argument, e.g. for and against homework, for and against eating meat, for and against eating sweets in class, for and against the use of cars. Stress that the object is not to express an opinion but to present the evidence fairly on both sides of the argument, leaving the readers to make up their minds.

Shared writing
Select one of the topics discussed in the whole-class session and make notes for a piece of writing, using this formula:
1. Presenting the issue
2. Arguments for
3. Arguments against
4. Concluding paragraph. (Explain that this can take one side or the other, argue that both points of view are wrong, argue that it doesn't matter, say that some ideas from both points of view are good or take a different view entirely.)

Independent writing
Ask children to work on a final draft of the writing started in the shared writing session.

Session 2

This session should cover:

★ a more complex structure for discursive writing.

Whole class
Read passage 1 *Which Route for the Bypass?*, then work on an outline of its structure, i.e.
• Introductory paragraph
• Points against the south route
• Points for the south route
• Points against the Owl Wood route
• How the effect on Owl Wood could be minimised if that route were chosen
• A paragraph to round off the argument.

Ask children to discuss why there is no paragraph explaining the advantages of the Owl Wood route, i.e. it is shorter and cheaper – this information is covered or implied elsewhere.

Compare this with the work done in session 1. There, a simple for and against argument was presented. In this session, two options, each with arguments for and against, is presented.

Shared writing
In the independent writing activity children will be asked to bullet the key points from each paragraph. Support this task now by working together on the 'points against the south route' paragraph.

Independent writing
Ask children to summarise the remainder of the text using bullet points.

Session 3

This session should cover:

★ writing texts putting forward a point of view.

Whole class
Read passage 2 *A Disastrous Idea,* discussing the key differences between this and passage 1, i.e. in passage 2 the writer has a point of view and wishes to persuade other people.

Compare passage 2 with the 'points against Owl Wood' in passage 1. What additional points does the writer of passage 2 make? Discuss how the arguments put forward in passage 2 could be countered by a supporter of the Owl Wood route, e.g. the road could be fenced, the wood could be extended, and so on. This could be done in then form of an improvised conversation.

Highlight any statements that are simply an opinion, e.g. the last paragraph.

Highlight words that are intended to influence the reader's emotions, e.g. peace and quiet, noisy, dangerous, destroy, killed, disaster.

Shared writing
Review the independent writing produced in session 1. Choose one, and work with the class on a plan for a piece of writing intended to persuade the reader, using emotive language and ignoring the other point of view.

Independent writing
Ask children to produce a final draft of the writing worked on in the shared writing activity. Confident writers could write a piece of persuasive writing of their own.

Topic

15 Language Change

GfW unit covered: 54

Objective: S2 (Term 3)

Grammar or language topics covered:

• Language change over time

● ●

Session 1

This session should cover:

★ word change.

Whole class

Read passage 1 *Five of the Clock,* explaining that it was written nearly 400 years ago. Discuss the overall meaning of the text, pointing out that people got up earlier and went to bed earlier in the seventeenth century, because of the lack of cheap lighting.

Work with the class to highlight unusual words. Use different colours to show words that have changed their spelling (e.g. schoole, merrilie), words that seemed to be used in a way that is different from modern usage (e.g. stored, herd, without, find) and words that are used little or not at all in modern writing, (e.g. fie, sluggards, apace, goeth, gotten, counsel).

Shared writing

Create a table for the various words highlighted, and discuss their modern equivalents.

Independent writing

Perhaps working in groups, ask children to produce a glossary of modern equivalents for the words.

Session 2

This session should cover:

★ stylistic changes in writing.

Whole class

Read passage 1 again, this time looking at overall aspects of style. Children should spot that the sentences are very long indeed, and there are some unusual grammatical constructions, e.g. 'the bells ring to prayer', 'if weather be fair', 'the servants at plough'.

Shared writing

Begin working a modern version of passage 1. Explain that not only will the words need to be changed, the grammar and style will need to be modernised too. The text might start: 'It is five o'clock. The sun is well up in the sky, and it is time for lazy people to get up!'

Discuss the final sentence, in which Nicholas Breton sums up the particular hour of the day. A modern version might be 'It is a time when work gets under way, and profits can be made.'

Independent writing
Ask children to work on modernising the remainder, or part of the remainder of the passage.

Session 3

This session should cover:
* ★ modern idiomatic language;
* ★ use of slang.

Whole class
Reread the passage included on page 15 (Tony's letter to Mike). Discuss the slang words and their 'standard English' equivalents, e.g. quid = pound, skint = having no money.

Discuss which words would not make sense to a sixteenth-century Elizabethan, e.g. CDs, £34.60, power cut. (If there is time, some of the slang words could be looked up in an etymological dictionary to discover their origin – e.g. 'quid' is first recorded as being used in 1688 to mean a sovereign.)

Now read passage 2 from this topic, *The Chart Show.* Highlight any slang or deliberately trendy words. What audience does the broadcaster have in mind? Have any of the words already become old fashioned? Why does standard English date more slowly than writing such as in passage 2? How does passage 2 differ from dialect?

Shared writing
Work on a table showing 'standard English' equivalents for the words in passage 2. Add any other contemporary (and possibly temporary) words and phrases known by the children.

Independent writing
Either ask children to rewrite the text in standard English, based on the work done in the shared writing activity, or ask them to write their own piece using current idioms. This task would be suitable only for the most confident children.

Alien Arrival

In a quiet valley outside town, strange lights were glowing, unseen by any human being. A door on the mysterious saucer-shaped craft was gradually opening. Inside, strange, tall figures were moving about.

At last two of the aliens stepped out. They were green, and very tall and thin, with small heads on very long necks. They looked around them with their single, yellow eye.

In the distance they could see a glow in the sky. This must be the lights of a city, and that was just what they were looking for!

The two creatures spoke to each other. Their voices were quiet, like the whispering of a breeze through the branches of a tree. They had spotted a path, and it seemed to lead towards the city!

They were soon on their way. Behind them, the saucer rose silently into the sky. The aliens liked the look of this planet. It was a pity that it was already inhabited by intelligent creatures, but they could be dealt with quite easily when the main force arrived. First they needed to check out the city, and to do that they needed an effective disguise. They mustn't be spotted!

A Warning to All Householders

All householders are warned that aliens have arrived during the night, and they are aiming to take over the world. Intelligence reports state that there are at least two aliens in the city.

It is believed that they are disguised as lampposts.

ACTION

All householders should immediately check the lampposts outside their property. Please remember that a simple visual check will not be sufficient as the aliens look exactly like real lampposts. However, it is understood that the aliens are very ticklish. Householders should:

1. Take a broom or garden tool with a long handle.
2. Tie or glue a large feather on the end.
3. Tickle each lamppost under the chin.

Should any lamppost start giggling, it is essential to contact the city council's Alien Disposal Department. Keep watch on the alien while you are waiting for the disposal engineers to arrive, in case it moves to another street.

Remember:

◆ Adverbs modify (add to the meaning of) verbs, e.g. she **slowly** woke up. They can also modify adjectives (the **very** angry teacher) and other adverbs (the train went **extremely** quickly).

◆ Adjectives modify nouns, e.g. the **tall** tree.

◆ A mixture of long and short sentences gives variety and adds interest to writing. Use punctuation and joining words to build sentences.

Topic 2 Active and Passive

A Tense Task (1)

Abdel looked through the shop window. Inside, a customer was being served by Mr Patel. Another customer was being looked after by Mr Patel's daughter Meera. They were both occupied by their work. Now was his chance!

Abdel strolled into the shop, looking as innocent as possible. The bag of sweets that had been stolen by Marcus was in his pocket. It was vital to put it back before its loss was discovered by Mr Patel. It was also important that Abdel wasn't seen replacing it by the shopkeeper. He might think it was being stolen by him!

The corner of the shop where the sweets were kept was hidden by a stand containing birthday cards. The sweets were quickly pulled out by the anxious boy. He bent down to put them back, then – disaster! The card stand was knocked over by Abdel's school bag! He could be seen by everyone in the shop!

A Tense Task (2)

Abdel looked through the shop window. Inside, Mr Patel was serving a customer. Mr Patel's daughter Meera was looking after another customer. Their work occupied both of them. Now was his chance!

Abel strolled into the shop, looking as innocent as possible. In his pocket was the bag of sweets Marcus had stolen.

One Thing After Another

It was a bad day for Vicki. First she had been told off by her mum when a plate had got broken at breakfast. Then she had been grumbled at by the bus driver because she only had a ten pound note in her purse.

Once the office had been reached by Vicki, she hoped things would improve. But her desk had been messed up by the cleaner and her computer was being mended by a technician. She was told by him that it had been affected by faulty software and wouldn't be fixed for an hour!

Then she was called in by her boss.

"I'm sorry, Vicki," she said. "The work done by you yesterday won't do! It will have to be done again!"

Remember:

♣ Most sentences use the active voice. Somebody or something does something, e.g. Will kicked the ball.

♣ In the passive voice somebody or something has something happen to them, e.g. The ball was kicked by Will.

♣ The passive voice is useful at times, but using it too often can make your writing sound awkward.

Topic 3

Connectives in Different Text Types

Mrs Turner's Plan

Mrs Turner was preparing for a busy day. The vicar and other important members of the village community were coming to tea. She wanted to make a very special cake!

Before starting she checked her cupboards for ingredients. Nothing vital was in short supply, so she was able to get started without having to visit the shop. Although she had only recently arrived in the village, she had a growing reputation for her wonderful cakes and she wanted this to be the best ever.

Once the ingredients were set out on the table, she reached for her trusty mixing bowl. Next she opened the bag of flour and carefully sieved the right quantity into it; sieving made her cakes lighter. She was ready for the sugar now, and she poured a cupful into the flour, stirring all the time. Then she added some butter, and as soon as it was thoroughly mixed in, she cracked three eggs into the bowl then began to stir, smoothly beating the eggs into the mixture.

After this she measured out three teaspoonfuls of ginger – double the usual quantity – vital as she wanted a strong flavour.

Finally she took a small bottle out of a locked cupboard and read the label carefully. 'Deadly poison,' it said. She poured it in, smiling. With all that ginger, they would never notice it.

How to Build a Website

Despite the fact that many people think that creating a website is difficult, anyone with experience in word processing should manage it easily. However, because there are millions of sites available on the worldwide web it is vital that your website makes an impact and is well designed.

First, create a home page with interesting text and graphics using a simple web-designing program such as Front Page Express. Because this is the first page people will see, it has to be interesting. Now create more pages, linking them to your home page with hyperlinks; your web-building programme will do this for you.

When your website is finished you will need a host for it; this is the computer that will make your website available for everyone to visit. Often, the ISP (Internet Service Provider) you use to send your emails and surf the web will provide space for your web pages. To upload your pages, you will need special software called an FTP (File Transfer Protocol) program. When your pages are uploaded, sit back and wait for visitors to arrive!

Remember:

- Joining words and phrases (connectives) can join short sentences to make long ones, and can link ideas from one sentence to another.
- One job of connectives is to show how events are ordered. **First, next, soon, at last, finally** are examples of this type of connective.

34

More Punctuation

An Obituary

Sir James Carstairs OBE, OM.

Sir James Carstairs, the well-known explorer who died yesterday, lived a life of great achievement. Despite his disability (he only had one arm following a childhood accident) he led expeditions to many countries: Bolivia, Borneo and Antarctica were the scenes of some of his greatest exploits.

What drove Sir James to continue exploring well into his sixties? His long-time assistant Henry – a native of Paraguay – put it this way.

"Sir James was always restless. He couldn't sit still for a minute; he was always looking for new places to explore."

One well-known story about Sir James involves a trip to the Pacific, where, following a storm, he survived for ten days in a small boat by drinking rainwater and catching flying fish!

In later years Sir James was active in the conservation movement; much of his time was spent campaigning to protect the rainforests. He was showered with awards: the OBE in 1985, a knighthood in 1991, and the Order of Merit in 2001.

Sir James, one of the greatest heroes of modern times, will be missed by all his family and friends. Lord Bolton, president of the Society of Explorers, gave this tribute:

"Sir James was a one-off. He was more than a friend, he was an inspiration; we shall all miss him."

Mad About Manchester

Terry, the boy in the picture, lives in Manchester, he loves the town and says he never wants to move away. Manchester City, his local team, is a great love, he attends as many matches as he can. They are not the most successful team in Manchester, that is Manchester United, so why does Terry support 'The Blues'. They need it more, says Terry.

Terry comes from a large family, four sisters, two brothers, and many aunts and uncles live with him or nearby. His father, a local police constable, shares Terry's enthusiasm for City, he is often on duty at matches and sees the games for free.

Terry's best friend Liam, not a City supporter, shares Terry's other great enthusiasm, fishing. Sometimes they fish where they are not supposed to, once they were caught, which was very embarrassing for Terry's father, as he was the policeman who caught them.

Remember:

◄ Commas can be used to separate different parts of a sentence. They help the reader work out when to pause.

◄ A semi-colon can be used to link clauses and sentences instead of a joining word, e.g. It was raining; I decided to stay at home.

◄ Colons are most often used to introduce lists, examples or quotations.

◄ Brackets and dashes are used to separate out words that are not really part of a sentence, e.g. Mr Brown (a teacher at the local school) was convicted of speeding last week.

5 Complex Sentences

Ready, Steady, GO!

Wiping sweat off their faces, the two teams in the final stared at each other. At last the moment of truth had arrived! On the signal, they lined up and lifted the rope. Undoubtedly the inter-village tug-of-war was the high point of the year.

Before he gave the signal to tug the referee spoke to both teams. He carefully explained the rules, although they knew them perfectly well. If the ribbon tied to the middle of the rope crossed either of the lines painted on the ground, the tug was over.

Tensely, the teams waited for the sound of the whistle. At last, the referee blew!

Everyone knew it was going to be a tough contest; Great Puddington had won for the last three years and were determined to make it four in a row. Little Puddington, the underdogs, had never reached the final before. Since last year some tough youngsters had moved into the village, so hopes were high of causing an upset.

Both teams strained and sweated. The ribbon started to move – towards the Little Puddington line! Desperately, Great Puddington dug their heels in and heaved. Nearer and near to the all-important line moved the ribbon. Ten centimetres . . . five centimetres . . . it was there! The whistle blew. Triumphantly, the Little Puddington team yelled "YES!" and jumped for joy. Ashamed and humiliated, Great Puddington slunk away.

A Crisis at the Zoo

The lion escaped from the truck. The truck had been bringing it to the zoo. The lion escaped with one bound. The zookeepers stared at it. They were horrified. The head keeper snatched up his mobile phone. He did this quickly. He asked for people with dart guns. They were busy dealing with another crisis. He asked for the police to come. The lion disappeared into the bushes. It wasn't hungry. It had just been fed. This was lucky. The keepers followed the lion. They didn't think of the danger. It was important to track the lion. They wouldn't know where it had gone if they didn't. They realised it was heading for the local primary school. The keepers were alarmed. The police had arrived. They contacted the primary school. The children were made to stay in the school. The doors were locked.

Remember

♣ There are many interesting ways to link parts of a sentence.

  – You can use a range of joining words.

  – You can use punctuation.

♣ You can arrange parts of the sentence in different ways.

♣ Always listen to your sentence and think about how it sounds.

♣ 'And' is only one way to join short sentences to make long ones. There are plenty of others!

Further Work on Active and Passive

Susan's Good Idea

The train had been stopped at a signal. The passengers were furious. They had been delayed for nearly an hour now. The problem had been caused by a derailment at Clapham Junction.

At last information was given over the public address system. The passengers were told that their train would end its journey at the next station. A bus had been hired to take them to London. The rail company was sorry, but the problem had been caused by circumstances beyond its control.

At last the train began to move. Susan was filled with gloom. Her interview was timed for 2.30. There was no hope of getting there now. Her chances of the best job in the world had been ruined!

Just then a thought struck her. She had a contact phone number. Mrs Peacock had said she could be rung up at any time.

The phone rang. It was answered by Mrs Peacock.

"Hello," said Susan. "It's me, Susan Sharpe. I'm stuck! A train has been derailed at Clapham Junction!"

"What train are you on?" asked Mrs Peacock.

"The 12.15 from Weybridge."

"Well, I am amazed!" said Mrs Peacock. "So am I! Come along to the buffet car and I'll meet you there. You can be interviewed on the train!"

Old House in the Hills

Whipped by cruel winds,
Raddled by relentless rain,
The tumbledown house was battered,
Bent, broken.

Years had been stretched to centuries,
Owners were forgotten,
Or overcome by death;
Slates had been ripped from the roof
Leaving holes like gaps in rotten teeth.

But thick wall had not been toppled,
The sky's eye
Was still jabbed by
The chimney's shaking finger,

Like an old man's
Dying defiance.

Dafydd Morgan-Jones

Remember:

● The passive voice can be used without saying 'who did it', e.g. It was agreed that the day had been a triumph. It can add variety to your writing.

A Reminder (1)

Mr M P Wickham
60 Tudor Rd
Mud-on-Sea
Dorset BH12 9GW

Wessex Power PLC
Spark House
BOURNEMOUTH
Dorset
BH 44 9GH
Our ref: DG/NW36

12 March 2003

Dear Mr Wickham,

Account 8769542XF19/5R

We are writing to you to remind you that there remains due an outstanding balance of thirty pounds and sixty-four pence on your electricity account.

This is the second communication sent to you concerning this matter, and we respectfully advise that, if sufficient funds to settle the account are not forthcoming within seven days of the above date, we will have no choice but to terminate the supply to your premises and take legal action to recover the outstanding balance. We remind you that our reconnection charge is one hundred pounds, plus VAT.

We look forward to your earliest attention in settling this matter.

Yours sincerely

Dianna Green (Mrs)
Finance Dept, Wessex Power PLC

A Reminder (2)

Dear Mike,

Hi! Di here from Wessex Power. Remember me? You owe us thirty quid! You'd better pay up quick or it's the big switch off for you, chum . . .

Remember:

◆ Formal language is used for official letters, to and from an organisation rather than a person.

◆ Formal language is used when you are writing to a person you do not know.

◆ You would use informal language when writing to a friend or close relative.

Contracting Sentences, Note Making

The History of the Parachute

The word parachute comes from two French words, 'parer', to avoid, and 'chute' a fall. The purpose of a parachute is to increase wind resistance so that a falling object can descend slowly and safely.

The parachute was first described by Leonardo da Vinci in about 1500. He drew a man attached to ropes beneath a pyramid-shaped parachute. No real experiments were made until 1777, when a French balloonist called Montgolfier dropped a live sheep attached to a parachute from a tower. The first human to jump with a parachute was another Frenchman, L.S. Lenormand who jumped from a tower in 1783.

Early parachutes were built like umbrellas with rigid ribs. In 1880 the first limp-canopied parachutes appeared, and in 1908 the modern parachute, carried in a pack and opened by ripcord, was invented. The first parachute jump from an aircraft took place in 1912.

In 1927 the Russians thought of using parachutes as a means of invading foreign countries. This idea was used in the Second World War and the 'paratrooper' was born.

Parachutes saved many pilot's lives in World War 2. However, faster aeroplanes meant that parachuting became difficult. By 1945 ejector seats were developed to throw pilots clear of the aircraft before the parachutes were opened.

Today parachuting, sometimes involving free falling from great heights, is a very popular sport.

Parachute Timeline

1500 – Leonard da Vinci draws 1st chute.
|
1777 – 1st parachutist – a French sheep.
|
1783 – 1st human parachutist – L.S. Lenormand jumps from tower.
|
1880 – Invention of limp-canopied chute.
|
1908 – Modern chute (folded in pack with ripcord) invented.
|
1912 – 1st jmp frm plane
|
1927 – Russians think of using 'paratroopers' for invasion.
|
1939-1945 WW2 – chutes save 1000s of lives. Xtnsive use of paratroops.
|
1945 – Ejector seats dvlpd.
|
Prsnt day – parachuting a pop. sport.

♣ Remember:

♣ **Note making** is making a list of the main points in a piece of writing.

To make notes, cut out as many words as you can. (Make sure your notes still make sense!)

♣ Abbreviations and shortened forms of words can be used.

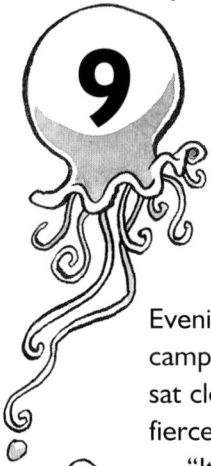

At the End of the Day (1)

Evening had come. The workers and most of the police officers had gone home. The protesters' camp was lit up with fires. It was early in the summer, and the nights were chilly. Lisa and Luke sat close to their fire, glad of the warmth. Lisa's dog, Raven, lay between them. Raven looked fierce and menacing, but he had never hurt anyone. He adored Lisa.

"It was incredible when the digger vanished down that hole!" said Lisa. "I'm glad the driver wasn't hurt!"

"It would have served him right if he had been, if you ask me," said Luke.

Lisa was more sympathetic. She knew that the digger driver was just an ordinary man, doing his job, even if they didn't agree with what he was doing. They thought back to the amazing events of the morning. When the big digger had moved further into the trench, the ground had given way. The machine had slid front-first into a great hole in the hillside. The driver had managed to scramble out. A chain had been fixed to the digger, and a giant dumper truck had been used to pull it out.

Work had stopped for the day. Nothing could be done until the hole was filled in. Local archaeologists said that the hole had to be examined first. The road builders were not pleased!

At the End of the Day (2)

Everyone had gone home by evening. The protestors had lit fires as it was chilly. Lisa, Luke and Raven the dog sat by a fire. Lisa and Luke talked about the day. A digger had fallen down a hole in the hillside. The driver wasn't hurt. Lisa was pleased, but Luke didn't care. A dumper truck had pulled the digger out. Archaeologists had to examine the hole before it was filled in. Work had to stop.

Remember:

🐙 Summarising is reducing a text to its most important points.

🐙 A summary is a shortened version of a text, not a set of notes.

Topic 10 Conditionals

How to Look After Your Qrrp

Qrrps are friendly animals from planet Squinge. They make excellent pets as long as they are looked after carefully.

Make sure that your Qrrp is fed properly. They will thrive on ordinary Earth-type dog food, but if you can provide them with living food now and again, such as spiders, they will be much happier.

Qrrps have scales rather than fur so they do not need grooming. However, if they stay too long in the sun they will get sunburn, so ensure that they are covered with sun cream before going out in the sun.

Qrrps are very noisy animals and unless you are prepared to put up with this do not choose one for a pet. They love singing, especially in the middle of the night and if you have neighbours you may need to soundproof your walls.

Qrrps need plenty of exercise, and if they are deprived of this they will become bad-tempered. As they have very sharp teeth and fangs it is sensible to keep them as happy as possible. Qrrps are quite large animals – a fully-grown male will reach a height of ten metres and a length of thirty metres. Unless your house is very large you may need to move; alternatively, you could build a Qrrp lair in your garden.

A Sulky Girl Wishes She Was the Sun

If I were the sun
I would shine brightly
To tempt you on to the beach,
Then I'd burn your skin bright pink;
If you refused to come out,
I'd shine through the window
Until you were dazzled.

If I were the sun, I would hide behind the clouds
All over the weekend,
Then come out shining when everyone was back at work;
If I saw you putting your washing out,
I would sulk,
And tell the rain to pour;
Then I would grin at you
With my silly bright face
As soon as you took it in again.

Remember:

◆ A conditional sentence shows one thing depends on another, e.g. If it rains tomorrow, I'm not going! The trip's off unless you behave!

◆ Conditional sentences contain words and phrases such as **if, unless, so long as, provided**.

◆ Conditional sentences often contain the word 'would', e.g. I would if I could.

41

Worried Sick

. . . Dad paced up and down the room. Why couldn't children do what they were told?

"Look at the time! Half past ten! And she's got an exam tomorrow! She's in big trouble when she gets in!" raged Dad. Mum said nothing, but her drawn, white face showed how worried she was. Tara had never been this late before.

Meanwhile, Tara was still plodding along the road that led to the village. She was furious with Lisa. Fancy telling her that the last bus ran at half past nine and only remembering it didn't run on Sundays when they had reached the bus stop! A five-mile walk was all she needed, with school tomorrow and a big exam. If only her mobile phone hadn't gone flat! And what would happen when she got home? She quickened her step. Dad was so short tempered! She would be grounded for a month!

Back at home, it was 11.30, and there was still no sign of Tara.

"I'm going to ring the police," said Dad. He was just about to pick up the phone when there was a sound outside the front door . . .

Late Night Bus Services

We are writing to you to complain about the bus service to Brunton Village. We hope you will consider improving it.

Punctuality

During the day, buses are meant to leave Abbeystock bus station at half past each hour, and arrive at Brunton at five past the hour. Often the bus does not leave Abbeystock until nearly a quarter to, and is consequently late in arriving at Brunton. This means that people living in Brunton who work or go to school there are often either late for work, or are forced to go on a bus an hour earlier.

Reliability

It seems that your bus company keeps its oldest buses for the Brunton route. Sometimes the bus breaks down on the way, and sometimes it doesn't run at all. Please remember that the bus is a life-line to villagers in Brunton as there is no other means of transport apart from cars. Children and old people do not have cars.

Late night services

Last bus to Brunton in the week: 9.30

Cinema and theatres in Abbeystock – performances finish after this.

Sundays – last bus 8.30

Remember:

🐚 In a story, a new paragraph shows a change of time or place.

🐚 A new paragraph is also used when someone new speaks.

🐚 In non-fiction, a new paragraph shows that the author is writing about a new topic.

🐚 Sometimes the paragraph can have a heading.

Judy's Journal

July 12th 2010

What a day it's been! It started like any other day, with me helping Dad with the harvest in the forty-acre meadow. We didn't hear it at first, as the noise of the combine is pretty loud, but as it got lower we heard it all right. Dad turned off the engine and jumped off the combine, and we stood there goggle-eyed as the giant silver saucer landed in the middle of the field. Luckily it landed where we had already cut the corn.

It was obviously a flying saucer, and when the door opened and the blue chap came out it was clear it hadn't come from anywhere on Earth. We didn't feel frightened at all – I expect we were just too astonished. Anyway, he was clearly perfectly friendly and he (or she) waved to us across the field. We walked over to him. He looked perfectly human – apart from being blue, that is.

Dad liked science fiction and he knew what to do. He pointed to his chest.

"Me Bill!" he said. Then (pointing to me) "this Judy! Welcome to Earth!"

But the blue creature spoke perfect English. "Good to meet you, Bill. We've been listening to your radio broadcasts and we know your language, so we don't need to go through all that 'me Bill' stuff. Now, listen, this is important. Did you know that your planet is in danger?"

We didn't, so we listened.

The Story of Christopher Columbus

Christopher Columbus set sail across the Atlantic Ocean on August 3rd, 1492, with three ships. The journey was longer than he imagined, and many members of the crew had begun to lose heart, and they demanded to return to Europe. However, by September they were beginning to see seabirds. This made them think they were approaching land. On October 11th a branch was sighted floating in the sea, and the following day land was sighted at last.

This was not America, but a small island in the Bahamas. Columbus landed and claimed it for Spain. Columbus called the friendly natives 'Indians' as he thought he had sailed right round the world and landed on an island near India!

Columbus went on to discover further islands, then returned to Spain. He was so sure that the islands he had discovered were near India he called them the 'West Indies' and they are still called this today.

Remember

- A recount tells a story. This might be fiction or non-fiction.
- In a recount, events take place one after another.
- A recount is normally written in the past tense.

Features of Instructional Texts

How to Use an Internet Search Engine

There are millions of websites on the internet. Search engines help you find the information you want by searching through all these pages for particular words and phrases selected by you.

1. Find your search engine. There is a wide range of search engines available. Some will allow you to select from websites from one country only. Others provide categories, such as sport or music, to make your search easier. Others even allow you to ask direct questions.

2. Now enter your key word or phrase in the search box. If you enter more then one word, you can use a capital AND. The search engine will only look for websites containing both words. If you use OR it will look for search engines with either word.

3. Read through the list of sites produced by the search engine. Not everything will be helpful.

4. If you don't find what you want, you will need to think of different search words to enter into the search engine.

5. Once you have found an interesting website, don't forget to check out any lists of links to other websites on a similar subject.

How to Attract Wild Birds to Your Garden

Would you like to attract different wild birds to you garden? Here's how!

First make sure that birds are safe in your garden by discouraging cats as much as you can. Next, provide plenty of cover; birds need bushes and trees in which they can shelter and build their nests. Birds require a wide range of nesting sites so it is important to provide a wide range of planting.

Water is important to birds, so include a water feature in your garden if possible. Birds will also need a source of food, so include plants that provide berries. A wild patch of garden will attract insects, which will provide food for insect-eating birds.

Give your birds a little extra help by putting out food in cold weather, and nesting boxes in the spring. Do not put out wild bird food in the spring – young birds need to learn to find their own wild food. Bird food is best placed on a bird table or in a hanging bird feeder – out of the reach of cats!

Remember:

◆ Instructional writing tells you how to do something.

◆ Instructional texts often are written in the order you need to do things, and use words like **first**, **next**, **finally**, and so on. With some jobs, such as making a wild bird garden, the order is not so important.

◆ Instructional writing uses the present tense.

Persuasive and Discursive Texts

Which Route for the Bypass?

A new bypass for West Green is essential. The streets of the town are choked with through traffic, and the situation in the High Street is dangerous for pedestrians. Two routes have been proposed; the south route, and the north route through Owl Wood.

The south route would be expensive, as it passes through an area of housing. Houses would have to be cleared away and people would lose their homes. West Green Manor, a seventeenth-century listed building, would have to be demolished. This route would also be two miles longer than the one through Owl Wood. However, it would provide additional access to the new industrial estate, which could then expand and provide much-needed local employment.

Owl Wood is an area of outstanding natural beauty, and wildlife and the environment would undoubtedly be damaged by a bypass. In particular, the colony of owls could be affected, and rare plants in the path of the road would have to be replanted.

These problems, however, could be minimised by careful landscaping, access tunnels for animals beneath the motorway, and good fencing to prevent animals wandering into the road. As part of the plan money could be put aside for further tree planting on the east side of the wood, extending it by over fifty hectares.

As we have said, a bypass is essential. It is now up to you to select the route.

A Disastrous Idea

I believe the government's plans to build the new bypass through Owl Wood is a disgrace.

Owl Wood is one of the last truly wild places in the area, and is listed as an area of outstanding natural beauty. Because of this, many people enjoy walking there at weekends and in the evening. Where else could they find such peace and quiet? It is also a valuable habit for plants and animals. The wood is famous for its owls, of course, but there are many other creatures found there, such as foxes and badgers. The wood is also one of the few places left where a rare orchid, the White Helleborine, still grows. Driving a noisy, dangerous dual carriageway through the heart of the wood would destroy all of this. Animals would be killed when crossing the road, and the extra disturbance would drive away the owls.

I believe that this road would be a disaster for the environment. I demand that the government immediately drops the whole idea.

Remember:

- ♣ Sometimes writing is used to argue a case. You would put all your best arguments to support your case, and then say why arguments against what you think are wrong.

- ♣ Sometimes a piece of writing can put both sides of a case. Often this sort of writing will end with the writer's opinion.

Five of the Clock

It is now five of the clock, and the sun is going apace upon his journey; and fie sluggards who would be asleepe: the bells ring to prayer, and the streets are full of people, and the highways are stored with travellers: the scholars are up and going to schoole, and the rods are readie for the truant's correction: the maids are at milking, and the servants at plough, and the wheel goeth merrilie, while the mistress is by; the capons and chickens must be served without door, and the hogs crie till they have their swill; the shepherd is almost gotten to his fold, and the herd begins to blow his horn through the town. The blind fiddler is up with his dance and his song, and the alehouse door is unlocked for good fellows; the hound begins to find after the hare, and horse and foot follow after the cry; the traveller now is well on his way, and if weather be fair, he walks with the better cheer: the carter merrilie whistles to his horse, and the boy with his sling casts stones at the crows: the lawyer now begins to look on his case, and if he giveth good counsel, he is worthie of his fee. In brief, not to stay to long upon it, I hold it the necessitie of labour, and the note of profit.

From *The Fantastics* by Nicholas Breton, 1626

The Chart Show

Hi! Yep, it's Craig Jones here, welcoming all you happenin' dudes to another wicked hour from the latest pop charts broadcast on 98.5 FM and on-line at www.popgoldfm.com forward slash chartshow. Remember, this is a phone-in show, so get on the old blower and give us a call on 01234 643879, or email us at craig@popgoldfm.com. First up is a dead funky new single from that totally cool band Banana Menace, You a-peel to me. We were all well gutted when the band threatened to split, but it turned out that was only show-biz spin. Right on! Take it away, Banana Menace!

Remember:

- Language changes with the passage of time. New words are being invented all the time, and people use grammar and punctuation in different ways.
- Words can change their meaning and spelling as time passes.